MAR 2011

Looking at
GROWING UP

HOW DO PEOPLE CHANGE?

Jackie Gaff

Enslow Elementary
an imprint of
Enslow Publishers, Inc.
40 Industrial Road
Box 398
Berkeley Heights, NJ 07922
USA

http://www.enslow.com

Enslow Elementary, an imprint of Enslow Publishers, Inc.

Enslow Elementary® is a registered trademark of Enslow Publishers, Inc.

This edition published in 2008 by Enslow Publishers, Inc.

Library of Congress Cataloging-in-Publication Data

Gaff, Jackie
  Looking at growing up : how do people change? / Jackie Gaff.
    p. cm. — (Looking at science : how things change)
  Summary: "A beginner's look at how people grow and change"—Provided by publisher.
  Includes bibliographical references and index.
  ISBN-13: 978-0-7660-3090-9
  ISBN-10: 0-7660-3090-3
  1. Human growth—Juvenile literature. 2. Developmental biology—Juvenile literature. I. Title.
  QP84.G22 2008
  612.6—dc22

                            2007024509

Printed in the United States of America

10 9 8 7 6 5 4 3 2 1

To Our Readers: We have done our best to make sure all Internet Addresses in this book were active and appropriate when we went to press. However, the author and the publisher have no control over and assume no liability for the material available on those Internet sites or on other Web sites they may link to. Any comments or suggestions can be sent by e-mail to comments@enslow.com or to the address on the back cover.

Every effort has been made to locate all copyright holders of material used in this book. If any errors or omissions have occurred, corrections will be made in future editions of this book.

For The Brown Reference Group plc
Project Editor: Sarah Eason
Designer: Paul Myerscough
Picture Researcher: Maria Joannou
Children's Publisher: Anne O'Daly

Photo and Illustration Credits: Alamy/Bubbles Photolibrary, p. 21B; Bananastock, pp. 1, 2; Corbis/Jose Luis Pelaez, Inc., p.26; The Brown Reference Group plc (illustrations), p. 17; Dreamstime, pp. 4, 8B, 13, 15T, 22, 30; istockphoto, pp. 6, 6B, 9B, 10B, 11T, 14, 18, 19T, 24, 25B, 26BL, 27B, 28, 29T; Paul Myerscough, pp. 8, 12B, 20B; Photos.com, pp. 23B, 27T; Shutterstock, pp. 5B, 10, 14B, 16, 16B, 18B, 20, 22B, 24B, 26BR; Geoff Ward (illustrations), p. 5.
Cover Photo: Bananastock

Contents

How do people grow?

A person grows taller and bigger as their body builds up bones, muscles, skin, and other parts.

◄ This boy is being measured to see how tall he has grown.

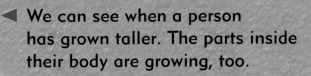

◄ We can see when a person has grown taller. The parts inside their body are growing, too.

As bones grow longer and bigger, the muscles around them grow, too. Other parts are also growing, including organs such as the brain, heart, and lungs.

It takes many ► years of growing before a child becomes an adult.

How do we begin to grow?

When an egg cell from the mother is joined by a sperm cell from the father, it begins to grow into a baby.

Babies grow inside their mother's womb, or uterus. In about nine months, the baby is ready to be born. People grow more quickly inside their mother's womb than at any other time of their lives.

How do babies grow?

Young babies eat and sleep
a lot. They grow very quickly.
By one year old, they may be
three times heavier than
they were at birth.

Babies kick their legs and
wave their arms. This
makes their muscles
grow stronger.

◀ By eight months old,
many babies can sit up.

By three months old, many babies can roll over. Next they learn to sit up, and then to crawl.

At about one ▶ year old most babies are learning to walk.

How do children grow?

Toddlers are babies over one year old who can walk.

Toddlers also grow very quickly. They learn how to move and balance. This helps them learn how to run and climb.

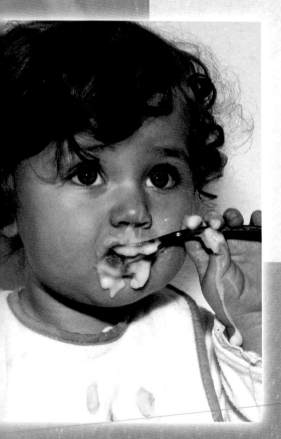

◄ Toddlers learn important skills as they grow, such as how to feed themselves.

Children also learn to communicate with others by talking. Their brains are growing, as well as the rest of their bodies.

▲ As children grow older, their muscles become stronger. They can learn to do more and more things.

How do teeth grow in?

Teeth are already growing inside a baby's gums while it is in its mother's womb. The teeth break through the gums a few months after the baby is born. Our first teeth are called "baby teeth" or "primary teeth."

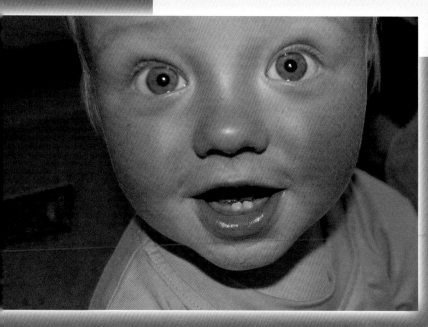

When children are about six or seven years old, their primary teeth start to fall out. Adult teeth take their place. Most children have about 20 primary teeth. Adults have about 32 adult teeth.

How does food help people grow?

Food contains energy, which people need to move their muscles and to grow. Bodies need a regular supply of energy. That is why it is important to eat three healthy meals every day.

Our bodies cannot work ▶ without water. People should drink six to eight glasses of water a day to stay healthy.

Our brain needs energy to think. Our lungs need energy to help us breathe.

Our heart needs energy to pump blood through our bodies.

Which foods are good to eat?

Healthy food contains vitamins and minerals. Our bodies need them to grow and to help make energy.

Healthy foods include fruits and vegetables, whole grain bread and pasta, fish, meat, and beans.

People need vitamins and minerals from many different foods to grow and stay healthy. A food pyramid shows how much of each type of food people should eat every day.

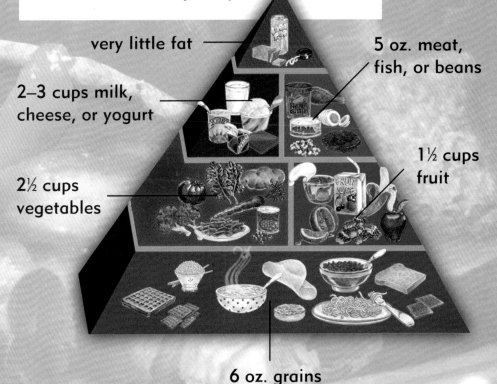

very little fat

5 oz. meat, fish, or beans

2–3 cups milk, cheese, or yogurt

1½ cups fruit

2½ cups vegetables

6 oz. grains

17

Why is exercise important?

When people exercise, they use their muscles. Muscles grow and become stronger every time they are used. The more a muscle is used, the stronger it becomes.

Everyone can keep healthy and strong by exercising.

People can stay ▶ fit and healthy by taking regular walks.

We need strong and healthy muscles to move, work, and play. Exercise also makes our bones, lungs, and heart work hard. That makes these body parts stronger and healthier too.

Why is sleep important?

When we sleep our bodies rest, heal, grow, and build up energy for the next day. It is important to go to bed at a regular time and get enough sleep.

▼ Young babies need to sleep about 18 hours a day to rest and help them grow.

Most young children need 10 to 12 hours of sleep every night. Adults need about 8 hours of sleep every night.

Reading a ▶ bedtime story can help children get ready to sleep.

How do children grow into adults?

Between the ages of 3 and 10, children grow steadily. Then they begin to grow very quickly again.

The bodies of ▶ these teens changed as they grew from children into young adults.

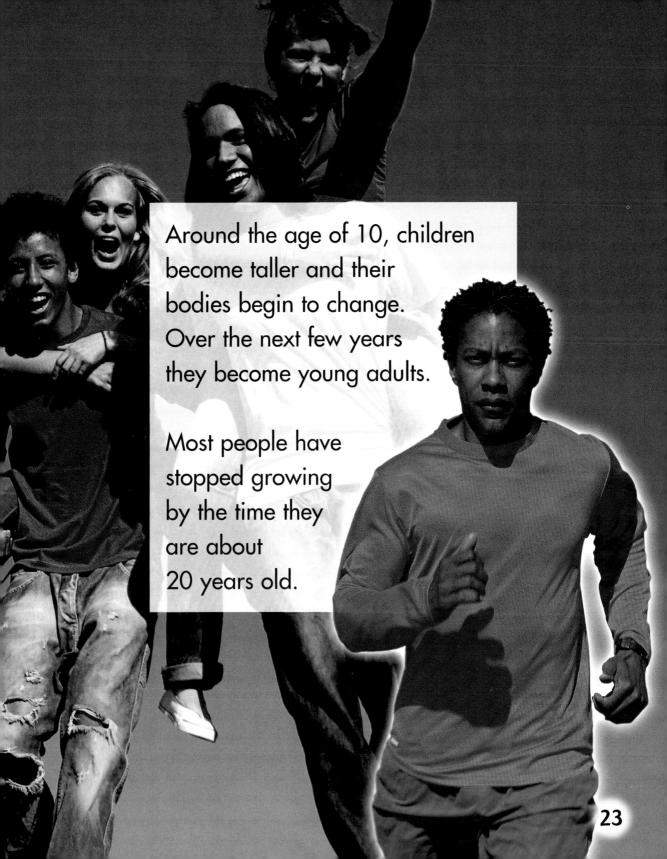

Around the age of 10, children become taller and their bodies begin to change. Over the next few years they become young adults.

Most people have stopped growing by the time they are about 20 years old.

23

How do adults grow older?

When people become adults, they may decide to have children of their own. As adults keep growing older over many years, their bodies keep changing.

Skin may become wrinkled as people grow old, and hair sometimes falls out.

▲ Older people may feel more tired. Their muscles can become weaker and they may need help to move around.

25

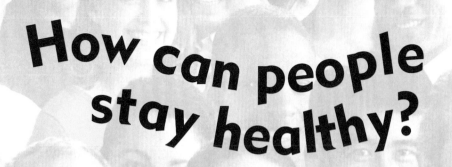

How can people stay healthy?

Our bodies grow when we eat healthy food, exercise, and get plenty of rest.

▼ People may look different, but our bodies all need healthy food, exercise, and rest to grow.

People who take care of their
bodies can help themselves
stay fit and healthy
throughout
their lives.

What do I know about growing up?

1. Keep a diary for a week.
Write down:

- How much exercise you got each day.

- How much of the following foods you ate each day: bread, vegetables, fruits, yogurt, cheese, fish, meat, rice or pasta.

- How much sleep you got each night. Did you sleep for 10 to 12 hours?

2. Look at photographs of yourself when you were a baby and a toddler. Then look in the mirror. In which ways has your body changed?

3. Keep a growth chart in your bedroom. Every month measure your height and write down how much taller you have grown.

4. Look at your teeth. Can you tell how many adult teeth and how many primary teeth you have?

Words to Know

bones — Hard parts of the body that help support muscles and organs.

brain — Organ that controls our bodies.

egg — Cell produced by the female that joins with a male's sperm to make a baby.

heart — Organ that pumps blood through the body.

lungs — Organs that help people breathe.

mineral — Substance found in food that our bodies need to stay healthy.

muscles — Parts of the body that help us move.

organs — Parts of the body, such as the heart or lungs, that carry out important jobs.

sperm — Cell produced by the male that joins with a female's egg cell to make a baby.

vitamin — Substance found in food that our bodies need to stay healthy.

womb — The uterus, the part of a woman's body where a baby grows before it is born.

Learn More

Books

Bullard, Lisa. *My Body: All About Me Head to Toe.* Minneapolis: Picture Window Books (2002).

Lobb, Janice. *Bump! Thump! How Do We Jump?* Boston: Kingfisher (2002).

Thomas, Pat. *My Amazing Body: A First Look at Health and Fitness.* New York: Barron's Educational (2001).

Web Sites

Brain Pop
www.brainpop.com/health/seeall/

KidsHealth
www.kidshealth.org/kid/body/mybody.html

Index